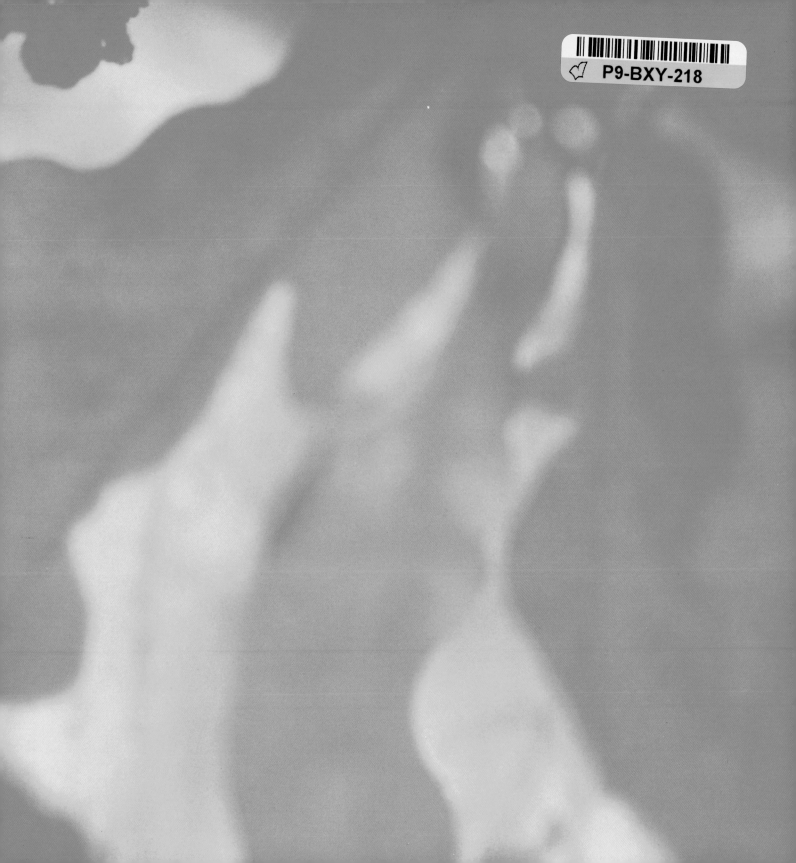

the autumn garden

a seasonal guide to making the most of your garden

the autumn garden

Richard Rosenfeld

LORENZ BOOKS

This edition is published by Lorenz Books

Lorenz Books is an imprint of Anness Publishing Limited
Hermes House, 88–89 Blackfriars Road, London SE1 8HA
tel. 020 7401 2077; fax 020 7633 9499
www.lorenzbooks.com/info@anness.com

© Anness Publishing Limited 2002

Published in the USA by Lorenz Books, Anness Publishing Inc.
27 West 20th Street, New York, NY 10011; fax 212 807 6813

Published in Australia by Lorenz Books, Anness Publishing Pty Ltd
tel. (02) 8920 8622; fax (02) 8920 8633

This edition distributed in the UK by Aurum Press Ltd
tel. 020 7637 3225; fax 020 7580 2469

This edition distributed in the USA by National Book Network
tel. 301 459 3366; fax 301 459 1705; www.nbnbooks.com

This edition distributed in Canada by General Publishing
tel. 416 445 3333; fax 416 445 5991; www.genpub.com

This edition distributed in New Zealand by David Bateman Ltd
tel. (09) 415 7664; fax (09) 415 8892

A CIP catalogue record for this book is available from the British Library.

10 9 8 7 6 5 4 3 2 1

Publisher: Joanna Lorenz
Managing Editor: Judith Simons
Senior Editor: Doreen Palamartschuk
Art Manager: Clare Reynolds
Additional text: Kathy Brown, Andrew Mikolajski and Peter McHoy
Designer: WhiteLight
Photographers: Peter Anderson, Jonathan Buckley, Michelle Garrett, Andrea Jones,
    Peter McHoy, Debbie Patterson and Steven Wooster.
Production Controller: Joanna King

page 1 Sedums produce a colourful show in autumn and are loved by bees.
page 2 *Stipa calamagrostis* makes a good companion for sedum in an autumn border.
page 3 Colchicums are among the most popular autumn-flowering bulbs.
page 4–5 Nothing beats the brilliant autumn foliage of the Japanese maple.

Note

In the directory section of this book, each plant is given a hardiness rating. The
temperature ranges are as follows:
frost tender – may be damaged by temperatures below 5°C (41°F);
half-hardy – can withstand temperatures down to 0°C (32°F);
frost hardy – can withstand temperatures down to -5°C (23°F);
fully hardy – can withstand temperatures down to -15°C (5°F).

CONTENTS

INTRODUCTION

You can pack plenty of bright vivid colours into the autumn garden. There are dozens of plants at their peak now, and the whole show can be set off by the even more spectacular "bonfire" of leaf colours as scores of deciduous trees and shrubs flare up red and orange and golden yellow. While it is tempting to think that the autumn garden should bow out gracefully with beautiful pale-coloured seedheads, which it can easily do with the right choice of plants, it can also end on a wonderful high with bold colours and brilliant displays.

left Many grasses are at their best in the autumn. The flowering spikelets turn beige and silvery and look attractive in the autumn sun.

right A smart autumn combination is richly coloured *Crocosmia* 'Lucifer' and golden brown *Helenium* 'Waldtraut'.

below *Sedum spectabile* provides a welcome burst of bright colour in the autumn garden. It attracts bees and butterflies, and livens up the front of a border.

THE KEY TO A LIVELY, RICHLY COLOURED AUTUMN garden is to make sure that it has a first-rate selection of bulbs, perennials, grasses, conifers, and, best of all, shrubs and trees that come into their own during this period. Those with an end of season "flare up" offer a rich array of purple and scarlet, with lashings of yellow and orange.

gumballs, maples and burnt sugar

The best way to find the most colourful autumn plants is to visit private and public gardens which have a superb autumn show. Identify the best plants, working in layers down from the trees to the ground. A liquidambar tree, like a flaming brand at 6m (20ft) high, might be far too big for most gardens but there is usually a lively alternative. *Liquidambar styraciflua* 'Gumball' has just as many colours but is a sensational shrubby mound, at just 2m (6ft) high.

Cultivars of the the Japanese maples (*Acer palmatum*) can be anything from 75cm (2½ft) to 8m (25ft) high and have a fantastic range of deep colours. One of the best for a medium-size garden is the slow-growing

'Crimson Queen', whose leaves turn reddish-purple, and it never exceeds 75cm (2½ft). If a maple does start getting too big for the garden, it can always be pruned to size. They look best when half the richly coloured leaves are still hanging on, giving views through bare branches to the rest of the garden, and half are lying like a radiant rug on the ground.

left *Acer palmatum* produces a brilliant display of scarlet leaves.

below The soft beige tones of *Cortaderia* blend in well with bolder autumnal colours.

Cercidiphyllum japonicum (katsura tree) is the autumn tree with a big difference because, as well as flamboyant colours, it has the terrific scent of burnt sugar and toffee apples. As the leaves start to fall they release a wonderful scent in a wide radius, up to 30m (100ft) away. The katsura tree needs to be given plenty of space to grow, because it can reach 6m (20ft) high after 20 years; if space really is quite restricted, prune it to one trunk because it often produces several stems.

grasses and perennials

The countryside in autumn is largely beige and brown as grasses start to fade, and the leaves of many trees start to crinkle, die and fall. Gardens need plenty of these colours as they inject a traditional low-key feel to the end of the year. They provide an essential link between the brighter summer colours and winter.

Some grasses, like pampas grass, have much more style though. *Cortaderia selloana* has gigantic late summer and early autumn feathery plumes. Most of the grasses can be left standing right through the autumn and winter before being cut back to be replaced by fresh new growth early the following spring. By leaving them unpruned, you will ensure that the garden has plenty of stems and seedheads to keep it architecturally alive right through the dormant season.

Other perennials will need cutting back at the end of autumn. *Sedum spectabile* (ice plant) flowers at the end of summer into early autumn, adding pink flowers which bring the autumn show of colours right down to the ground. With a wide, imaginative planting of bulbs such as colchicums, nerines and sternbergias, you can guarantee a richly coloured garden, in all hues, from the evergreens to loud bursts of magenta red with patches of soft and gentle beige.

AUTUMN PLANTS

The following pages provide a selection of the best autumn plants. They include bulbs, perennials, grasses, shrubs, climbers, trees and conifers. Start by planting a few in each category and then, over the following years, begin filling in the gaps, creating some powerful eye-catching autumn colours in different areas of the garden, and more low-key, gentler colours in other parts. Look to see which plants thrive best in the conditions in your garden, and you can gradually build up a beautiful autumn display.

left Rudbeckias provide some of the brightest autumn colours with their vivid yellow flowers. Most have a distinctive central disc. Easy to grow, they thrive in a hot, sunny position.

bulbs

There is a small select group of highly desirable bulbs for the end of the year. They provide a beautiful contrast to the more brazen shows of colour on the trees and shrubs, and help keep the eye moving around the garden. Most require well-drained soil and plenty of sun in order to thrive, though there are some that prefer shady, moist conditions. Do not remove the foliage until it has turned brown, or next year's display will suffer.

Canna

Commonly known as Indian shot plants, or Indian reed flowers, these are exotic plants for the autumn garden. Even if they did not flower, they would be worth growing for their large, smooth leaves. Use them with grasses and brilliant dahlias to bring the season to a close with a flourish. Stictly speaking they are rhizomatous perennials, but they are planted like bulbs. They are excellent in large containers.

C. hybrids

The cannas grown in gardens are hybrids, of which there are many. All the following have green leaves unless otherwise indicated. All are half-hardy. 'Black Knight' has dark red flowers and bronze leaves. 'Brandywine' has scarlet red-orange flowers. 'City of Portland' has yellow-edged, rose pink flowers. 'Ingeborg' has salmon pink flowers and bronze leaves. The free-flowering 'Lucifer' has yellow-edged crimson flowers. 'Orchid' has pink flowers. 'President' has bright red flowers. The flowers of 'Primrose Yellow' are pale yellow. 'Richard Wallace' has canary yellow flowers. 'Rosemond Coles' has yellow-edged, bright red flowers. The orange flowers of 'Wyoming' are frilled and have darker orange edges; the leaves are bronze. Smaller cannas can be planted together in groups, but do not overcrowd them and allow room for their leaves to develop. The taller cannas can be used as individual specimens, providing the focal point of a bright display.
Flowering height To 2m (6ft)
Flowering time Midsummer to early autumn
Hardiness Half-hardy

below left *Canna* 'Brandywine'.

below right Many canna hybrids have dramatically coloured leaves, such as *C.* 'Assaut', which are deep purple.

opposite left *Colchicum speciosum* 'Album'.

opposite right *Colchicum speciosum*.

Colchicum

These pretty bulbs are often known as autumn crocus, or naked ladies (or naked boys in the United States). The flowers of colchicums are always a surprise when they appear, and it is easy to forget that the corms are in the garden. The leaves, large and glossy, do not appear until the following spring (the best time to transplant them, if this is necessary). They are excellent in light woodland or planted around shrubs. In borders the leaves can be a nuisance in the spring. Robust types are also excellent for naturalizing in grass. *C. speciosum* is the most widely grown member of the genus, and produces goblet-shaped, pink flowers in autumn. 'Album' has 1 to 3 goblet-shaped, weather-resistant, white flowers that are green at the base. It is a good plant in open ground in borders or grassland. *C.* 'The Giant' is one of many hybrids, with large, lilac-pink flowers. Plant them in light shade, for example beneath deciduous trees and on the sunny side of shrubs.

Flowering height To 15cm (6in)

Flowering time Autumn

Hardiness Mostly fully hardy

above left to right
Crocosmia x *crocosmiiflora*
'Emily McKenzie', *Nerine bowdenii* and *Crocosmia* x *crocosmiiflora* 'Solfatare'.

opposite left Cyclamen thrive in rich soil in dappled shade under trees or shrubs.

opposite right *Sternbergia lutea.*

below *Cyclamen hederifolium.*

Crocosmia

These colourful perennials are originally from South Africa. Excellent as they are as border plants, combining well with roses and annuals, they also look effective when grown in isolation in large groups. The leaves are linear, lance-shaped, mainly ribbed and about 60–100cm (2–3ft) long. The flowers are excellent for cutting. *C.* x *crocosmiiflora* (montbretia) is a hybrid group including many garden-worthy forms. They can be grown just about anywhere in the garden, provided they are given sun or light shade, and fertile soil. They can be used to arch over the edge of a pond, their reflections caught in the water, to soften the edge of a straight path, and to provide a colourful contrast next to an evergreen shrub. The key to a good show is a bold group of corms clustered close together so that they have plenty of impact. 'Emily McKenzie' has orange flowers with brown throats from late summer to autumn. Also flowering from late summer to autumn, 'Solfatare' produces a succession of apricot-yellow flowers among its grassy, bronze-tinged leaves. 'Jackanapes' has tri-coloured, orange, red and yellow flowers.
Flowering height To 1.5m (5ft)
Flowering time Late summer to autumn
Hardiness Fully hardy

Cyclamen

The genus includes 19 species of tuberous perennials, found in a wide variety of habitats from the eastern Mediterranean to North Africa and the Middle East. The rounded to heart-shaped leaves often have attractive silver markings. They like well-drained, humus-rich soil in sun or partial shade.

C. hederifolium

This species was formerly known as *C. neapolitanum*. The pink flowers have a darker red stain towards the mouth. The pretty ivy- or heart-shaped leaves are often patterned. *C. mirabile* has pale pink flowers with serrated petals and purple-stained mouths. The leaves are heart-shaped and patterned with silver blotches.
Flowering height 10cm (4in)
Flowering time Autumn
Hardiness Fully hardy

Nerine

This is a genus of about 30 species of bulbs found on well-drained mountainous sites in Africa. The common name, Guernsey lily, is properly applied to *N. sarniensis*. The flowers appear in the autumn, followed by the leaves in late winter, and the plant goes dormant in summer, when it likes a dry, warm period. They

flower best when the bulbs are packed quite close together. *N. bowdenii* has umbels of up to 7 or more funnel-shaped, slightly scented, pink flowers, each to 7.5cm (3in) across, with wavy-edged, recurved petals, borne on stout stems. It must have a well-drained site and is a good choice for the foot of a sunny wall, where the pink flowers look striking. In cold areas, provide a dry mulch in winter.

Flowering height 45cm (18in)
Flowering time Autumn
Hardiness Fully hardy

Sternbergia

This genus of 8 species of dwarf bulb is found on hillsides, scrub and pine forests in southern Europe, Turkey and central Asia. They are similar to crocuses but have 6, not 3, stamens and grow from bulbs rather than corms. Like the crocus, some species are autumn-flowering, and some flower in spring. All parts are poisonous. They need hot sun and well-drained soil that dries out in summer. *S. lutea* has yellow, goblet-shaped flowers, 4cm (1½in) across, that appear at the same time as the dark green, strap-like leaves.

Flowering height 15cm (6in)
Flowering time Autumn
Hardiness Frost hardy

above left to right *Aster ericoides* 'Pink Clouds', *A. x frikartii* 'Mönch' and *A. laterifolius*.

perennials

Just when most summer perennials are well past their best, and getting ready for the dormant season, a few others are actually about to peak. The following, especially the asters, provide some of the best plants for the garden at any time of the year, let alone the autumn. They add a bright range of colours and shades, giving the border a much needed end-of-season lift.

Aster

This large genus includes the well-known Michaelmas daisies, essential plants for the autumn garden, many of which flower from late summer until the first frosts. Most also last well as cut flowers. The species are as worthy of consideration as the hybrids, some of which have an annoying tendency towards mildew (although all those described are trouble-free). The genus also includes annuals. Asters will grow in any reasonably fertile soil, in sun or light shade. Some will do well in poor soil. The taller forms often benefit from staking, especially in sites where they are exposed to strong wind, which can easily spoil them.

below *Aster turbellinus.*

A. ericoides

The species, which is native to North America, has given rise to several garden-worthy forms. They have wiry stems that are starred with flowers, all with yellow centres, in autumn. 'Blue Star' has pale blue flowers; 'Golden Spray' has white flowers; 'Pink Cloud' has light mauve-pink flowers.
Flowering height 75cm (30in)
Flowering time Late summer to late autumn
Hardiness Fully hardy

A. x frikartii

This group of vigorous hybrids includes some of the best of the Michaelmas daisies, all with a long flowering season. 'Mönch' is an outstanding selection, which has large, lavender-blue flowers carried freely on branching stems. It is an excellent companion to shrubby lavateras. 'Wonder of Stafa' usually needs staking and has pinkish-blue flowers.
Flowering height 75cm (30in)
Flowering time Late summer to early autumn
Hardiness Fully hardy

A. laterifolius

The species has an unusual habit: the erect stems produce flowering sideshoots, almost at right angles, giving a tiered effect. The flowers are white to pale lilac. 'Horizontalis', which is rather more spreading, has pale lilac flowers. The coppery tinges acquired by its dainty leaves as the weather turns colder enhance the appeal of the plant.
Flowering height 90cm (3ft)
Flowering time Midsummer to mid-autumn
Hardiness Fully hardy

A. novi-belgii

Although generally applied to the whole genus, strictly the common name, Michaelmas daisy, belongs to this species alone, the parent of a bewildering number of garden forms. It is often found growing as a weed, brightening up railway cuttings and areas of rough land with its violet-blue flowers in early autumn, which suggests a use in a wild garden or grass. The colours of the garden forms range from white, through all shades of pink, to pale and dark lavender-blue and some purples. They vary in height from dwarf forms, which are good at the edge of a border, to more substantial plants. One of the best of the taller varieties is 'Climax', which has pale lavender-blue flowers in early autumn. Among the good dwarf forms are 'Jenny', which has purplish-red flowers, and 'Lady in Blue', which has lavender-blue flowers.

Flowering height 30cm–1.5m (1–5ft)
Flowering time Late summer to mid-autumn
Hardiness Fully hardy

A. turbinellus

A refined-looking species from the United States, this has wiry stems that carry violet-blue daisies in autumn.

Flowering height To 1.2m (4ft)
Flowering time Early to mid-autumn
Hardiness Fully hardy

Helenium

These valuable daisy-like flowers are easily grown and merit a place in any border planned for autumn interest. Together with dahlias and chrysanthemums, they bring a warm glow to the garden at the end of the season, and they look good with a range of grasses. The following hybrids all flower from late summer to mid-autumn. 'Indianersommer' has rich golden-yellow flowers; 'Moerheim Beauty', one of the best known, has rich brownish-red flowers that age lighter brown; 'The Bishop' has yellow flowers with dark eyes.

Flowering height To 1.5m (5ft)
Flowering time Midsummer to autumn
Hardiness Fully hardy

Physalis alkekengi

Commonly known as the Chinese lantern, this is a good plant in the cottage garden. The orange, papery shells surrounding the fruit are excellent for use in dried arrangements. During winter the shells slowly disintegrate, leaving only the veins and exposing the fruit within a wiry skeleton cage. Plant in well-drained soil, in full sun. *P. peruviana* is known as Cape gooseberry.

Flowering height To 2m (6ft)
Flowering time Midsummer (late summer to autumn seedheads)
Hardiness Fully hardy

above right *Aster novae-angliae* 'Purple Dome'.

below left to right
Helenium 'Indianersommer', *Physalis alkekengi* and *Helenium* 'Waldtraut' with *Crocosmia* 'Lucifer'.

above *Rudbeckia fulgida.*

Rudbeckia

Coneflowers are easy to grow, sturdy and essential plants for borders in early autumn. The petals of the daisy-like flowers droop away from the contrasting centres in an appealing way. They combine well with grasses. *R. fulgida*, or black-eyed Susan, is an excellent garden plant. *R. fulgida* var. *sullivantii* 'Goldsturm' has large, richer yellow flowerheads. *R.* 'Goldquelle' has double flowers with yellow petals and greenish centres.
Flowering height To 2m (6ft)
Flowering time Late summer to autumn
Hardiness Fully hardy

Schizostylis

Kaffir lilies will brighten up the autumn and early winter garden with their elegant spikes of fresh-looking flowers. Since they spread rapidly, regular division is advisable. There are a number of desirable selections. *S. coccinea* looks like a small gladiolus, with slender, grassy leaves and spikes of cup-shaped, red flowers. Among the many cultivars are 'Major' (syn. 'Grandiflora'), which has bright clear red flowers; 'Sunrise' (syn. 'Sunset'), with salmon pink flowers; and 'Viscountess Byng', one of the last to flower, with pale pink flowers.
Flowering height 60cm (2ft)
Flowering time Late summer to early winter
Hardiness Frost hardy

Sedum

These reliable plants have broad heads of sweetly-scented pink to mauve flowers that attract bees and butterflies. They need a sunny site, and their fleshy leaves enable them to tolerate drought. The genus also includes small species for the rock garden.

S. 'Herbstfreude'

This robust hybrid is the best-known of all sedums. It has large, fleshy grey-green leaves and heads of scented flowers in the autumn, deep pink at first, turning to salmon-pink and aging to a dramatic, rich brick-red.
Flowering height 60cm (2ft)
Flowering time Early autumn
Hardiness Fully hardy

S. spectabile

Probably one of the parents of 'Herbstfreude', this species is commonly known as the ice plant. It is roughly similar to the hybrid but is smaller and has pinkish-mauve flowers. Among the many cultivars are *S. s.* 'Iceberg', which is a good white. *S. s.* 'Brilliant' produces an abundance of bright rose-pink flowers from late summer to autumn.
Flowering height 45cm (18in)
Flowering time Late summer to early autumn
Hardiness Fully hardy

right *Sedum* 'Herbstfreude'.

far right *Sedum spectabile.*

Zauschneria

Often called Californian fuchsia, this genus of sun-loving perennials provides brilliant material for the front of a border, the funnel-shaped flowers being a vivid scarlet in most cases. They are best with the shelter of a warm wall in cold areas, where they are not reliably hardy. They also thrive and look spectacular when growing on the sunny side of a dry stone wall. Their key requirement is excellent drainage.

They can be grown in gravel gardens, especially in areas with low rainfall. *Z. californica* is the best-known species, and has attractive, lance-shaped, grey-green leaves, the perfect foil to the luminous scarlet flowers, produced from late summer to early autumn. 'Dublin' has slightly longer, bright orange-red flowers.

Flowering height To 30cm (12in)
Flowering time Late summer to early autumn
Hardiness Frost hardy

top left *Schizostylis coccinea,*
top right *Sedum spectabile*
'Iceberg', **bottom left**
Sedum spectabile,
and **bottom right**
Zauschneria californica.

above *Cortaderia selloana albolineata.*

below *Stipa gigantea.*

top right *Hordeum jubatum.*
below right *Molinia caerulea.*

grasses

Ornamental grasses are excellent for providing shape and structure throughout autumn and winter – the flowering heads can be left standing until spring. Some are imposing plants that make impressive specimens, give height to borders or provide accents, while others can create soft, feathery drifts to soften any colour scheme. Some bamboos make good screens, as well as providing useful stakes. All the grasses described, unless otherwise indicated, like a well-drained site in full sun.

Cortaderia

Commonly known as pampas grass, there are about 24 species of evergreen, tussock-forming grasses in the genus. Their coloured, glistening plumes can be a decorative feature in autumn or winter when covered with frost. Always wear gloves and take care when cutting back the plants in spring: the leaves are lethally sharp. *C. selloana* 'Sunningdale Silver' is an outstanding form, with plumes of silver-cream flowers in late summer and autumn.
Flowering height 3m (10ft)
Flowering time Late summer to early autumn
Hardiness Mostly fully hardy

Hordeum

Commonly known as barley, the genus contains 20 species of annuals and perennials, including *H. vulgare*, the well-known cereal crop, which are mainly of interest to the gardener because of their flowers. They are splendid additions to late summer and autumn borders, combining well with dahlias and Michaelmas daisies. *H. jubatum* (foxtail barley or squirrel-tail barley), from north-eastern Asia and North America, is an attractive annual grass. The showy plumes of straw-coloured flowers appear in late summer and early autumn, making this excellent for filling gaps in borders towards the end of the season.

Flowering height 50cm (20in)
Flowering time Late summer to early autumn
Hardiness Fully hardy

Miscanthus

These elegant perennial grasses are handsome enough to serve as specimens, besides their other uses in beds and borders and for cutting. They develop pleasing russet tints in the autumn. *M. sinensis* is a clump-forming species from eastern Asia with bluish-green leaves and pale grey spikelets, tinged with purple, in the autumn. 'Gracillimus' (maiden grass) is tall, with narrow leaves, which curl at the tips, and plumes of buff-yellow flowers in the autumn. One of the most attractive selections is 'Kleine Fontäne', which produces upright clumps of leaves and heads of pale pink flowers.
Flowering height To 2.4m (8ft)
Flowering time Late summer to autumn
Hardiness Fully hardy

Molinia

These are graceful perennial grasses that look delightful in herbaceous and mixed borders. They like moist but well-drained soil, preferably acid, in sun or partial shade. *M. caerulea* (purple moor grass) is a species from Europe and south-western Asia and has green foliage that turns yellow in the autumn. Upright stems

are topped with purplish flowerheads from late summer to autumn. *M. caerulea* subsp. *caerulea* 'Variegata' is an elegant form, with green and white striped leaves, which are sometimes tinged pink, and loose purple-grey flowers on arching stems in late summer and autumn.
Flowering height To 1.5m (5ft)
Flowering time Spring to autumn
Hardiness Fully hardy

Phyllostachys

The 80 or so evergreen bamboos in the genus are elegant enough for use as specimens in large gardens, or at the back of large borders as a backdrop to other plants. They like moist but well-drained soil in full sun or partial shade. Mature specimens of the imposing *P. bambusoides* (giant timber bamboo) have thick green canes that can be used for building. It has copious, broad, glossy, dark green leaves. *P. b.* 'Allgold' (syn. 'Holochrysa', 'Sulphurea') has golden-yellow canes, sometimes striped with green. *P. nigra* (black bamboo) is a Chinese species with canes that become black with age, a good contrast to the abundant green leaves.
Height To 7.5m (25ft)
Hardiness Fully hardy

Stipa

Commonly known as feather or needle grass, these are lovely grasses that make fine border plants. *S. arundinacea* (pheasant's tail grass) is an excellent grass for the autumn garden, a New Zealand species with long, tawny-beige foliage that intensifies in colour as the temperature drops. Thin stems carry brownish flowers in late summer. *S. calamagrostis* is good for planting in drifts. With its narrow, arching leaves, it blends happily with a range of plants. The silky flower-heads, which appear in summer, are initially green with a reddish tinge, fading to golden-yellow in late summer.
Flowering height 1m (3ft)
Flowering time Summer to autumn
Hardiness Fully hardy

above *Stipa calamagrostis.*

below *Phyllostachys bambusoides* 'Castilloni'.

below left *Miscanthus.*

shrubs

Many shrubs produce a wonderful display of autumn foliage or an eye-catching show of berries. Hungry birds might strip the branches of berries quite quickly, but with luck many will hang on through winter. Other shrubs look good when they have been topiarized and some can even be pruned so that they have striking bare legs with all the attractive leafy growth at the top.

Abelia

These evergreens are greatly valued for their graceful habit and late flowers, which last from midsummer to late autumn. They like well-drained soil in full sun, preferably against a wall in cold areas. *A.* x *grandiflora* is of garden origin and has slightly scented, white flowers from midsummer to autumn. 'Gold Spot' (syn. 'Aurea', 'Gold Strike', 'Goldsport') has greenish-yellow leaves.
Height To 2m (6ft)
Flowering time Summer and autumn
Hardiness Frost hardy

below left to right
Abelia x *grandiflora*, *Berberis temolaica* and *Abelia* x *grandiflora* 'Gold Spot'.

Abutilon

These elegant shrubs produce appealing lampshade-like flowers from late summer into autumn. They are sometimes trained as standards and used as dot plants in park bedding schemes. They are also good in containers, either on their own or as a central feature in a mixed planting. They need a well-drained site in full sun. *A. megapotanicum*, a trailing abutilon, is an evergreen or semi-evergreen species with orange-red and yellow, lantern-like flowers and maple-like leaves. The leaves of *A. m.* 'Variegatum' are mottled with yellow. This makes a good standard.
Height To 5m (16ft)
Flowering time Late summer to autumn
Hardiness Half or frost hardy

Berberis

An important genus, barberry is tough and hardy, and includes both evergreens and deciduous species, all with spiny stems. Although some are almost too familiar as hedging, there are also some very choice species that are well worth seeking out. The forms with coloured leaves make excellent specimens, but

beware of the sharp spines. They like well-drained soil and can tolerate partial shade, but produce better autumn colour and berries in full sun. Overgrown and straggly plants can be cut back in spring.

B. temolaica

A very handsome deciduous berberis, this slow-growing plant is difficult to propagate but is well worth looking out for. It has glaucous green leaves on whitened stems, lemon-yellow spring flowers and egg-shaped, crimson autumn fruits. Plants can be cut back hard annually or every two years for the interest of the winter stems.

Height 1.5m (5ft)
Flowering time Late spring (autumn berries)
Hardiness Fully hardy

B. thunbergii

This variable deciduous shrub has a number of interesting selections, all of which do best in fertile soil. The purple leaves of *B. thunbergii* f. *atropurpurea* turn orange in autumn. 'Aurea' has soft yellow leaves and is best in some shade. 'Helmond Pillar' is a distinctive upright selection with dark purple-red leaves. The popular and distinctive 'Rose Glow' has purple leaves swirled with pink and cream turning lipstick red in autumn. On 'Silver Beauty', the leaves are mottled with creamy white.

Height To 1.5m (5ft)
Flowering time Mid-spring (summer and autumn berries)
Hardiness Fully hardy

Calluna vulgaris

There are many excellent kinds of heather, which are often best used in groups to make a tapestry of colours and undulating shapes. They like an open site in full sun, with well-drained, humus-rich, acid soil. 'Arran Gold' has purple flowers and bright golden-yellow foliage, which turns lime green flecked with red in winter. 'Dark Beauty' has blood-red flowers and dark green foliage. 'Darkness' has deep crimson-pink flowers and mid-green foliage.

Height To 60cm (2ft)
Flowering time Midsummer to late autumn
Hardiness Fully hardy

above left to right *Berberis thunbergii* f. *atropurpurea*, *Abutilon megapotanicum* 'Variegatum' and *Calluna vulgaris* 'Arran Gold'.

below *Calluna vulgaris* 'Darkness'.

below Smoke bush.

Cotinus

Commonly called smoke bush, there are two species of impressive deciduous shrubs in the genus. The purple-leaved forms have spectacular autumn colour. They make large, rangy shrubs, but can be cut back hard for larger leaves, albeit at the expense of the flowers. The flowers are tiny, but carried in large panicles, looking like smoke from a distance – hence the common name. They are produced reliably only in hot summers. In cold areas it is better to cut the plant back hard annually for an improved foliage display. The purple-leaved forms are indispensable in a red or purple border. *C. coggygria* is the plain green species. Far better known is the selection 'Royal Purple', grown principally for its coin-like, dramatic purple leaves, which turn vivid red in the autumn. *C.* 'Grace' is similar to *C. coggygria* 'Royal Purple', but is larger and has oval leaves, which turn dark brownish-red in the autumn.

Height To 5m (16ft)

Flowering time Midsummer (autumn foliage)

Hardiness Fully hardy

Cotoneaster

This is an important shrub genus, containing both evergreen and deciduous species. Cotoneasters are tough, hardy, tolerant plants, which make excellent foils to a huge range of other showier plants. There are scores of different cotoneasters, in all sizes from 30cm (12in) to large shrubs and trees. Bees appreciate their creamy-white flowers in early summer, and birds enjoy their autumn berries. *C. dammeri*, an evergreen or semi-evergreen species, is an outstanding ground cover plant, carpeting the ground and thriving in many difficult garden situations. The plant flowers in early summer and bears scarlet berries in autumn. *C. frigidus* 'Cornubia' is a tree-like shrub, bearing bright red fruit in autumn, which is good enough to use as a specimen in a small garden. *C. horizontalis* is a versatile deciduous species, which can be grown as a wall shrub (or even up a tree trunk) or allowed to cascade over a bank, both of which methods display its unusual 'herringbone' habit. It has excellent autumn leaf colour, along with an impressive display of vivid red berries. *C. lacteus* is a dense shrub with an abundant crop of early summer flowers followed by orange-red berries. It is excellent hedging material.

Height To 3m (10ft)

Flowering time Spring to summer (autumn berries)

Hardiness Fully hardy

Enkianthus perulatus

Grow this plant for the small white flowers which appear in the spring, but better still, the superb flame red autumn foliage. It likes moist, well-drained, humus-rich soil, preferably acid, in sun or partial shade.

Height To 2m (6ft)

Flowering time Mid-spring (autumn foliage)

Hardiness Fully hardy

Erica

Also known as heathers, these are the familiar heaths, scrubby plants that can be used to carpet large tracts of land. They form the largest genus of heaths (the other two are *Calluna* and *Daboecia*), with some 700 or more evergreen species, and are particularly valued in the autumn and winter garden, although there are species that flower at other times of year. In smaller gardens, ericas are excellent in island beds, either on their own (or with *Calluna* and *Daboecia*) or with dwarf conifers, with which they associate happily. They are also ideal container plants. Most types of heather need acid soil, but unlike most of the summer-flowering heathers, those described here will tolerate alkaline soil.

E. carnea

Alpine or winter heath. This is an important species of carpeting heaths. The flowering season is from late autumn to mid-spring, with plants in milder climates being as much as two months earlier than those in colder areas. Generally they are in flower for six to eight weeks. They like well-drained soil in sun or partial shade. The following selections of cultivars are all hardy. 'Aurea' has pink flowers and gold foliage tipped with orange in spring. 'Fiddler's Gold' has bronze foliage and pink flowers. 'Golden Starlet' has white flowers and glowing yellow foliage, which turns lime green in winter. 'Myretoun Ruby' (syn. 'Myreton Ruby') has pink flowers, which turn magenta then crimson, and dark green foliage. 'Rosy Gem' has lilac-pink flowers and dark green foliage. The vigorous 'Springwood White' has white flowers. 'Westwood Yellow' has shell-pink flowers initially that darken to lilac-pink, and yellow foliage throughout the year.

Height 15cm (6in)
Flowering time Late autumn to spring
Hardiness Fully hardy

E. vagans

Cornish heath or wandering heath. A vigorous, evergreen, bushy species that provides flowers in autumn (some selections coming into flower in late summer). Regular pruning after flowering will keep plants neat, though the faded flowers, if left on the plant, will turn an attractive russet brown in winter. 'Kervensis Alba' has white flowers. 'Summertime' has shell-pink flowers. 'Valerie Proudley' has sparse, white flowers and bright lemon-yellow foliage.

Height To 80cm (32in)
Flowering time Midsummer to mid-autumn
Hardiness Fully hardy

below left to right *Erica vagans* 'Valerie Proudley', *E. carnea* 'Rosy Gem' and *E. c.* 'Fiddler's Gold'.

above Bright red leaves of *Euonymus alatus*.

below left to right
Euonymus with bright red berries, *E. fortunei* 'Emerald 'n' Gold' and the deep pink berries of *Gaultheria angustifolia*.

Euonymus

Commonly known as a spindle tree, the genus includes about 175 species of deciduous, semi-evergreen and evergreen shrubs, trees and climbers. The evergreen shrubs make excellent ground cover and some can even climb walls. Deciduous types have both spectacular autumn leaf colour and showy fruits. They like well-drained soil in full sun or light shade; evergreen shrubs need protection from cold winds.

E. alatus

A deciduous shrub with distinguishing bluish-purple autumn fruits. They split to reveal bright orange seeds at the same time as the leaves redden, but persist on the branches for a while after the leaves have fallen. It is suitable for a wild garden or in a hedgerow-type planting and will ultimately make a fine specimen.
Height 2m (6ft)
Flowering time Early summer (autumn foliage)
Hardiness Fully hardy

E. fortunei

This evergreen is exclusively grown in its variegated forms, of which there are a great many. The following are all hardy. 'Emerald 'n' Gold' has leaves edged yellow. 'Harlequin' is a dwarf plant, with mottled white and green leaves, useful as ground cover if planted in groups. Most handsome of all is 'Silver Queen', which has leaves broadly edged with creamy white. It is slow-growing but worthwhile and spectacular as a climber, more if wall-trained.
Height 90cm (3ft)
Flowering time Early summer (autumn foliage)
Hardiness Fully hardy

Gaultheria

There are about 170 species of these evergreen shrubs with alternate, quite leathery leaves and small bell- or urn-shaped flowers. In the autumn they produce quite large, spherical berries. They can be planted in heather and rock gardens, and are also suitable for woodland gardens. They need moist, peaty, acid soil in partial shade. The fruits are edible, but other parts of the plant can cause mild stomach upsets. *G. mucronata* (syn. *Pernettya mucronata*) is a compact shrub. It produces nodding white, or sometimes pink-flushed, flowers in late spring to summer. In autumn, fruits or berries appear, in various shades from white to purple-red.
Height To 1.2m (4ft)
Flowering time Early summer (autumn berries)
Hardiness Mostly fully hardy

Photinia

These excellent shrubs are grown mainly for the brilliance of their spring foliage. They suit a mixed or shrub border and make a good alternative to pieris in gardens with alkaline soil. *P. davidiana* is a handsome shrub, semi-evergreen in all but the coldest areas. Its long-lasting crimson berries ripen in autumn. Some of the leaves turn bright red at the same time, while others remain green. *P. x fraseri* is a hybrid group including many excellent selected forms. The new growth of the spreading form 'Birmingham' is deep coppery red. 'Red Robin' has spectacular bright red young stems and leaves in vivid contrast to the glossy green older leaves.

Height 3m (10ft)
Flowering time Spring and summer (autumn berries)
Hardiness Fully hardy

Pyracantha

Firethorn is an important genus of tough, hardy, spiny, evergreen plants that need some protection from cold wind. Impressive yellow, orange or red berries that last all autumn and winter follow the cream-coloured flowers cascading from the branches in summer. A highly effective use for pyracanthas is as a hedge. *P. coccinea* 'Red Column' is an upright shrub with reddish shoots and vivid red autumn berries, and shows excellent resistance to fireblight. *P.* 'Knap Hill Lemon' is an unusual variety, worth growing for its clear yellow berries. *P.* 'Soleil d'Or' is a popular hybrid with hawthorn-like white flowers in late spring succeeded by golden-yellow berries in the autumn.

Height To 3m (10ft)
Flowering time Early summer (autumn berries)
Hardiness Fully hardy to frost hardy

Skimmia

This small genus includes several attractive shrubs, which bear scented flowers in spring and (on female plants) red berries in autumn, a fine contrast to the handsome, evergreen leaves. They are excellent in shrub or mixed borders or containers. They need moist, well-drained, humus-rich soil; most prefer shade. Young specimens of the male *S. japonica* 'Rubella' can be used in winter window boxes. *S. x confusa* 'Kew Green', a male selection with fragrant, cream flowers in early spring, tolerates full sun. *S. japonica* is the most widely grown species. It has distinctive narrow, glossy foliage and panicles of cream buds throughout winter that open to fragrant creamy-white flowers in spring. 'Rubella' is a male form with clusters of red buds through winter that open to dingy white flowers in early spring. 'Tansley Gem' is a female form, with a good crop of red berries.

Height To 6m (20ft)
Flowering time Spring (late summer and autumn berries)
Hardiness Fully hardy

above left to right
Photinia davidiana, berries of *Pyracantha coccinea* 'Red Column', and *Skimmia japonica* 'Redruth'.

below *Pyracantha* (firethorn) with autumn berrries.

climbers

above Fluffy clematis seedheads provide an attractive autumnal display.

Many autumn climbers provide flashy leaf colours before the foliage falls, as well as late season flowers, and extraordinary seedheads. And, of course, there are some excellent evergreens, which provide a beautiful contrast to fiery, deciduous foliage, and are especially welcome once that has fallen. Climbers can be grown up a wide variety of supports, including pillars and posts, trellises, walls (to which supporting wires have been attached if necessary), and trees.

Clematis

There are clematis varieties that flower in spring, summer and autumn. As well as those with autumn flowers, all have beautiful, long-lasting seedheads, like silvery tassels of silk. They look best when they catch the sun, often in early morning when they are covered by a few drops of dew. They have varied cultivation requirements, but all like moist, fertile, well-drained soil and most clematis prefer full sun. 'Bill Mackenzie' has bright yellow, thick-textured, lantern-like autumn flowers, which are followed by fluffy seedheads.
Height To 7m (23ft)
Flowering time All seasons, depending on variety
Hardiness Mostly fully hardy

below left to right
Clematis 'Bill Mackenzie' flowers and seedheads with an underplanting of fuchsia, *Hedera helix* 'Parsley Crested', and *Clematis tangutica,* flowers and seedheads.

C. tangutica
This species produces bright yellow, lantern-like flowers with pointed sepals and a prominent central boss of stamens, which are borne from midsummer to autumn and are followed by silky, silvery grey seedheads. There is much confusion between this species and the roughly similar *C. tibetana,* which will hybridize with it freely.
Height To 6m (20ft)
Flowering time Midsummer to autumn
Hardiness Fully hardy

Hedera
These self-clinging, evergreen climbers are among the most useful of garden plants. Though the species *H. helix* can be too rampant, it has many desirable cultivars which are more manageable. With their glossy leaves, all ivies provide excellent evergreen cover for trellis, walls and fences, and can also do well as ground cover in the dry soil under trees where little else will grow. Another attractive use is trailing over banks or climbing up poles and gates. From a design point of view, evergreen climbers form part of the garden structure, around which the rest of the garden changes. Ivies tolerate a range of conditions. Green varieties are happy in shade, but variegated types need more light and protection from cold winds.

H. helix

'Dragon Claw' is an attractive ivy with large, broad, five-lobed leaves, curling downwards, with closely fluted edges that turn red in winter. It is good for growing up walls and for ground cover. 'Parsley Crested' has rounded leaves that are crested at the edges and turn a beautiful bronze in cold weather. The long, strong-growing trailing stems make this a good ivy for flower arranging and hanging baskets. It looks good in a conservatory growing up a pillar or growing over an archway. 'Perkeo' has unusual puckered leaves that are light green and turn light red in cold weather; it is borderline hardy. 'Spetchley' is the smallest ivy available. Its small, three-lobed variable leaves, sometimes triangular, grow very densely. One of its main attractions is that the foliage changes with the first frost to a lovely wine colour. 'Spetchley' is a really hardy ivy. It grows best outdoors, either in a container or in the open garden.

Height To 10m (33ft)

Hardiness Mostly fully hardy

Parthenocissus

These foliage plants are grown mainly for their spectacular autumn colour. All the species described here cling by means of suckering pads and are excellent on walls. They need fertile, well-drained soil in shade or sun. *P. henryana* is sometimes called Chinese Virginia creeper. It has dark green leaves that are distinctively marked with central silvery white veins; they turn red in autumn. It grows to 10m (30ft) and is borderline hardy. *P. quinquefolia*, Virginia creeper, has vivid flame-red autumn leaf colour. It is eye-catching as cover for a large wall, and can also be dramatic weaving through the branches of a large tree, such as a silver birch.

Height To 15m (50ft)

Flowering time Summer (autumn foliage)

Hardiness Borderline to fully hardy

Vitis vinifera

Tenturier grape is the parent of the many varieties grown for edible crops and also of a number of purely ornamental selections. *V. v.* 'Purpurea' is one of the most widely grown. The leaves mature to purple, then develop even richer hues in the autumn as the blackish, unpalatable fruits ripen. This is excellent for growing up an average size wall. For larger walls, the rampant, vigorous *V. coignetiae* will reach a height of 15m (50ft). Vines like well-drained, neutral to alkaline, humus-rich soil in sun or partial shade.

Height 7.5m (25ft)

Flowering time Summer (autumn foliage)

Hardiness Fully hardy

above *Parthenocissus henryana* beginning to turn red at the start of autumn.

below left to right *Hedera helix* 'Spetchley', the red foliage of *Parthenocissus* and *Vitis vinifera* 'Purpurea'.

below *Acer palmatum dissectum* 'Red Pygmy'.

trees

Autumn is an exciting season for trees: many deciduous ones offer sensational effects from richly coloured leaves, to brightly coloured berries, and those with attractive bark become more noticeable once they lose their leaves. Most medium-size gardens should have room for at least one kind.

Acer

Maples belong to a huge and important genus. There is one for every garden, large or small. *A. pseudo-platanus* (sycamore) is almost a weed in some gardens, but that should not blind you to the beauties of the other species. Maples suit a woodland planting or lightly shaded area, with fertile, well-drained soil.

A. griseum

A native of China, this slow-growing species is one of the most outstanding members of a fine genus. The leaves turn a brilliant red before they fall in autumn, but the principal interest is the cinnamon-red bark, which peels to reveal a richer colour beneath.
Height 10m (33ft)
Flowering time Spring (autumn foliage)
Hardiness Fully hardy

A. palmatum

Commonly known as Japanese maple, the species, which is native to Korea and China as well as to Japan, is a rounded tree or shrub displaying glorious autumn colour. *A. palmatum* f. *atropurpureum* (syn. 'Atropurpureum') is notable for the vibrant purple of its leaves, in spring and autumn. *A. palmatum* var. *dissectum* makes a dome-shaped tree with elegant ferny foliage, which turns red or yellow in autumn. It has a number of cultivars with coloured or variegated leaves. Acers in the Dissectum Atropurpureum Group have similar colouring to *A. palmatum* f. *atropurpureum* but with very finely dissected leaves, giving the plant a more filigree appearance. Slow-growing, they eventually make attractive, dome-shaped, spreading trees. 'Dissectum Nigrum' (syn. 'Ever Red') has finely dissected, blackish-purple leaves and forms a low, rounded bush. 'Fireglow' (syn. 'Effegi') carries rich burgundy-red leaves, which turn orange-red in the autumn. This requires some sun to enhance the leaf colour. 'Kagiri-Nishiki' (syn. 'Roseomarginatum') has pale green leaves margined with pink, later turning cream. 'Katsura' has the typical palm-shaped leaves of the species. Pale orange-yellow when young, they mature to a rich bronze, then redden in autumn. 'Ôsakazuki' carries mid-green leaves, which turn brilliant orange, crimson and scarlet in autumn. The red-tinted leaves of 'Rubrum' turn bright red in autumn. 'Sekimori' has very finely divided, filigree foliage, which is bright green, turning red or yellow in autumn.
Height 75cm–8m (2½–25ft)
Flowering time Spring (autumn foliage)
Hardiness Fully hardy

opposite, left to right top row *Acer palmatum* 'Fireglow', *A. palmatum* f. *atropurpureum* and *A. p.* 'Ôsakazuki', **middle row** *A. p.* 'Sekimori', the bark of *A. griseum* and *A. palmatum* 'Karasugawa', **bottom row** *A. p.* 'Bloodgood', *A. p.* var. *dissectum* and *A. x conspicuum* 'Phoenix'.

Arbutus

A genus with many attractions, not the least of which are the charming, strawberry-like fruits that give the trees their common name of strawberry tree. (The fruits are edible, if insipid.) The lily-of-the-valley-like flowers, which appear at the same time as the ripening fruits, are also beautiful. Add peeling bark to the list of attractions, and the surprise is that they are not more widely planted. There are two main reasons for this: not all are reliably hardy, and some will grow well only in acid soil; they need shelter and full sun. *A. unedo* is an evergreen species that has a spreading, sometimes shrubby habit. It is native to south-eastern Europe and the Middle East. The white flowers appear in the autumn, at the same time as the strawberry-like fruits from the previous year ripen. The red-brown bark, which peels in shreds, is also an attractive feature. The form *A. u.* f. *rubra* reaches the same size as the species, but has deep pink flowers.
Height 6m (20ft)
Flowering time Autumn (autumn fruit)
Hardiness Mostly fully hardy

Cercidiphyllum

The genus contains a single species, which is native to western China and Japan. It is a choice tree for the garden grown for its spectacular autumn foliage. These trees do best in woodland conditions – in fertile soil in light dappled shade – and although they are tolerant of lime, the best autumn colour occurs on acid soil. *C. japonicum* var. *magnificum* (syn. *C. magnificum*), or the katsura tree, is a rare Japanese upright species with rounded leaves that turn yellow,

orange and red in autumn and winter and smell of toffee and burnt sugar when they fall to the ground. As the leaves start to fall they release a wonderful scent in a wide radius, up to 30m (100ft) away. It needs plenty of room, as it can reach 10m (33ft) high after 20 years; if it produces several stems, you can prune it to just one to limit its spread.
Height 10m (33ft)
Flowering time Spring (autumn foliage)
Hardiness Fully hardy

Cornus

Dogwoods are among the best trees for a small garden. Some are grown for their overall appearance and so make good specimens, while others have striking spring flowers and good autumn leaf colour. The genus also includes many shrubs and a few perennials. The different varieties suit a range of soils and locations.
Height To 10m (33ft)
Flowering time Late spring and early summer
  (autumn foliage)
Hardiness Fully hardy

Crataegus

Despite their ubiquity as roadside plants, hawthorns make excellent garden trees, particularly in exposed situations and on poor, limy soils. They are tough and hardy, in sun or partial shade, and make excellent hedges, particularly in country gardens.
Height To 12m (40ft)
Flowering time Late spring and early summer
  (autumn berries)
Hardiness Fully hardy

Ilex

Indispensable plants in any garden for their healthy, glossy leaves, the hollies are either trees or shrubs depending on age and how they have been pruned (if at all). If you inherit a garden with a large holly, think twice before ousting it – it will undoubtedly be of venerable age. Holly also makes an excellent hedge. Berries will be produced only on females, which will need a pollinating male nearby, so choose carefully among the cultivars. Those listed here are evergreen. *I. aquifolium*, native to northern Africa and western Asia as well as to Europe, often appears in gardens, but the many cultivars generally make more attractive plants. The following selections are all hardy. 'Aurea Marginata Pendula' is a slow-growing, rounded, weeping tree with purple stems and spiny, glossy, bright green leaves, margined with creamy yellow. It is a female form, producing red berries in autumn. It is an outstanding plant for year-round interest. The male 'Ferox Argentea' carries very prickly dark green leaves margined with cream. 'J. C. van Tol' is self-fertile, with bright red berries among the plain leaves.

'Silver Milkmaid', a female cultivar, has an open habit and leaves with white margins. The berries are scarlet. 'Silver Queen' (syn. 'Silver King'), which is a slow-growing male form, also has white-edged leaves. It has a dense, upright habit. All hollies can be shaped and topiarized; try vertical cylinders or pyramids. They can also be grown as windbreaks or provide shelter. Variegated forms prefer full sun.

Height To 25m (80ft)

Flowering time Spring to early summer (autumn berries)

Hardiness Fully hardy

Liquidambar styraciflua

A superb large tree for one of the best displays of autumn foliage colour. Plant it in an open area, where it can be seen from windows in the house. It likes moist, well-drained, acid to neutral soil; it produces the best leaf colour in full sun.

Height To 25m (80ft)

Flowering time Late spring (autumn foliage)

Hardiness Fully hardy

above *Liquidambar styraciflua* produces a brilliant display of russet autumn leaf colour.

below Bright red berries of *Ilex aquifolium* 'J. C. van Tol'.

above *Quercus* leaves.

gardens. They like moist, well-drained soil, preferably in full sun. In spring *M.* 'Evereste', a conical small hybrid, bears a profusion of large white flowers, opening from reddish-pink buds. The fruits, which develop in the autumn as the leaves turn yellow, are bright orange to red.

Height To 12m (40ft)
Flowering time Late spring (autumn fruits)
Hardiness Fully hardy

Quercus

All the oaks are magnificent trees, and you shouldn't be put off by their final size. They stay small for quite a long time and can be pollarded to keep them within bounds, even if this prevents them from achieving their full splendour. Oak trees are important for wildlife, providing shelter for an enormous range of insects, birds and small mammals. Oaks should be grown in ordinary, well-drained soil, preferably in a sunny, open site. They tolerate light shade, but need space to expand. *Q. ilex*, a majestic evergreen, does particularly well in coastal situations. The variable leaves, often lance-shaped, are silver-grey when young, darkening to a glossy green as they age.

Malus

As well as all the apple trees (forms of *Malus domestica*), this genus includes the delightful crab apple. Though grown mainly for their ornamental value, crab apples can be cooked or made into jellies, and the trees make good pollinators for apple trees. They are compact and look good in cottage-style

right *Malus* 'Evereste'.

far right *Malus* 'Golden Hornet'.

Q. robur, the common English oak, is a large species with the characteristically lobed leaves and clusters of acorns in autumn. More manageable in smaller gardens are some of the selections, including the shrubby 'Compacta', which is very slow growing. Also slow growing is 'Concordia' (golden oak), a small, rounded form carrying bright yellow-green leaves in spring. The neatly upright 'Hungaria' resembles *Populus nigra* 'Italica' (Lombardy poplar) in outline.
Height To 30m (100ft)
Flowering time Late spring and early summer (autumn foliage and acorns)
Hardiness Fully hardy

Sorbus

The rowans are splendid plants for cold gardens. They are hardy and provide valuable berries for birds in winter. Attractive flowers and outstanding autumn colour add to their appeal. Most prefer moist, well-drained neutral to acid soil, in sun or light shade, but *S. aria* tolerates dry, chalky soil.

S. aria

A large number of cultivars have been developed from this European species. 'Lutescens' has a more conical habit than the species and is thus better suited to small gardens. The leaves are covered in creamy-white hairs and are particularly brilliant as they emerge in spring. The heads of white flowers that appear in late spring are followed by dark red berries.

Height 10m (33ft)
Flowering time Late spring (autumn berries)
Hardiness Fully hardy

S. commixta

This compact tree, from Korea and Japan, is generally grown in the form 'Embley', which fruits rather more freely. The white spring flowers are followed by an abundance of brilliant orange-red berries at the same time as the leaves turn red.
Height 10m (33ft)
Flowering time Late spring (autumn berries)
Hardiness Fully hardy

S. mougeotii

This unusual small tree or shrub is native to mountainous regions of northern Europe. The broad leaves have greyish hairs on their undersides. The fruits, sometimes lightly speckled, turn red in autumn.
Height 4m (13ft)
Flowering time Late spring (autumn berries)
Hardiness Fully hardy

Stewartia monodelpha

A deciduous tree or shrub with peeling, grey and red-brown bark. The leaves give a superb autumn display when they turn red and orange before falling.
Height To 25m (80ft)
Flowering time Midsummer (autumn foliage)
Hardiness Fully hardy

above left to right
Sorbus hupehensis, S. mougeotii and *Stewartia monodelpha.*

below *Sorbus* with autumn berries.

conifers

Once the summer flowers are over, conifers come into their own, both as a contrast to the colours of deciduous trees and shrubs, and later as welcome green features through the winter. There is a conifer for every size garden; they vary from neat, mounded dwarf forms, slow-growing, slim-line vertical trees which eventually reach 3m (10ft) high, to others with beautiful grey-blue foliage to monsters which grow 30m (100ft) high. They can be used to provide a wide range of effects including windbreaks on the garden boundary, ornamentals for their shape and coloured foliage, and architectural features adding extra interest from autumn to spring. They can be very effective in formal Italian or Eastern-style gardens.

Cryptomeria

Despite the common name, Japanese cedar, this monotypic genus (there is only one species) is found in China as well as Japan, albeit in two distinct forms. Japanese cedars will tolerate pruning and can even be coppiced or trained. They look good in Eastern or Japanese-style gardens, especially when they are grown to develop a gnarled trunk. Japanese cedars are among the most beautiful of all the conifers.

C. japonica

The species can reach a height of 25m (80ft) and is roughly columnar in shape. There are a huge number of cultivars available, suitable either as specimens or for use in rock gardens. All are hardy. 'Bandai-Sugi' is a slow-growing rounded dwarf form with blue-green foliage that bronzes well in cold winters. The intriguing 'Cristata' (syn. 'Sekka-sugi') has leaves that are curiously fused together, so that they resemble coral. 'Elegans' is potentially large and will form a broad obelisk; the trunk is often attractively curved. The wedge-shaped leaves are soft and bluish-green when young, turning a rich, glowing bronze in autumn. 'Lobbii' makes a handsome specimen in a large garden, forming a tall, slender, conical tree. The needle-like leaves are arranged in spirals. On mature specimens the thick, fibrous bark peels away. The cones age to brown. Rich, fertile soil is best, though they also grow on chalk. Prune in spring if necessary.
Height To 25m (80ft)
Hardiness Fully hardy

Taxodium

Swamp cypresses are among the most elegant of all conifers. Unfortunately, their eventual size rules them out for all but the largest gardens. They like moist or wet, preferably acid soil in full or partial shade. *T.*

distichum is a large, deciduous (though sometimes semi-evergreen) conifer that comes from the south-eastern United States. It forms a tall cone shape that becomes untidy as it matures. The needle-like leaves, which redden in the autumn producing an excellent display, are carried in two ranks. Mature plants produce the best colour. Purple male cones hang down and are a feature in winter; the female cones are inconspicuous. Near water it produces special breathing roots, which look like knees emerging from the ground around the trunk.
Height 40m (130ft)
Hardiness Fully hardy

Taxus

Yews are a valuable genus of conifers for the garden, with a range of foliage colour and habit. It grows in any well-drained, fertile soil, in sun or deep shade. Yew is widely used for hedging and topiary work, since, unlike most other conifers, it tolerates pruning and even seems to thrive on it. Even mature specimens will recover well if cut back hard. These conifers produce fleshy berries (usually red) rather than woody cones, which help to brighten up autumn and winter gardens. All parts are toxic; in some areas, there are restrictions on planting, particularly where cattle are being grazed.

T. baccata

A long-lived conifer, this is widely found in Europe and also in North Africa and Iran. Typically, it has blackish-green leaves, carried in a comb-like arrangement on the stems; male and female flowers are produced on separate plants, with berries, each containing a single seed, following on the females. Uncut, the yew forms a broad, spreading cone shape with dense horizontal branches, if unpruned. *T. b.* 'Lutea' has yellow berries. 'Fastigiata' (Irish yew), a female (and hence berry-producing) selection, is a familiar graveyard tree, forming an obelisk, pointed at the crown, but spreading with age. The stems are strongly upright. It can be kept within bounds by pruning and can also be wired into a narrower, more formal shape. It is an excellent choice for the small garden due to its limited size. It makes a good container plant. Yew also makes an excellent clean-cut hedge with nicely clipped sides, and various topiary shapes. They include everything from abstract geometric shapes to birds and beasts.
Height To 20m (70ft)
Hardiness Fully hardy

Thuja

These excellent conifers are similar to *Chamaecyparis* and are often mistaken for them, a distinction being that *Thuja* has aromatic foliage. They are just as good for hedging. Varieties include a number of coloured foliage forms. They like deep, moist, well-drained soil in full sun, and need shelter from very cold winds.

T. occidentalis

Although northern white cedar is not widely grown, it is the parent of a vast number of cultivars. 'Ericoides', a dwarf form, grows into a broad, sometimes rounded, obelisk. The spreading, scale-like leaves are green in summer, turning rich brown, sometimes purple, in autumn. As the name suggests, it combines well with heathers and is good in a rock garden.
Height To 20m (70ft)
Hardiness Fully hardy

T. orientalis 'Aurea Nana'

This is an appealing dwarf selection of a much larger species from China and Iran. It makes an egg-shaped plant, with yellowish-green, scale-like leaves held in irregular, vertical, fan-like plates; they tinge bronze in cold weather in autumn. The cones are flagon-like and bluish-green, maturing to grey. An excellent choice for a small garden, it associates well with heathers and other yellow-leaved shrubs. It can be grown in large pots or tubs, in old kitchen sinks, raised beds and rock gardens. It is so slow growing that even after many years it is unlikely to reach its full height.
Height 60cm (2ft)
Hardiness Fully hardy

AUTUMN DISPLAYS

You can create all kinds of effects in the autumn garden, from the quiet and gently atmospheric to the bold and bright. The scores of berries that start appearing now on shrubs and trees will, with luck, be with you until midwinter, keeping the garden interesting and colourful. Autumn is a marvellous time for reassessing the garden, and starting to make plans for the new year. It is the time to fill gaps where you need more late season interest and plant trees, shrubs and hedging, as well as bulbs that will flower the following spring.

left A beautiful glade of Japanese maples with a stunning display of foliage colour in bright reds, burnt oranges and golden yellow hues.

right One of the most exciting ways to use coloured foliage is near the edge of a pond or stream, where the colours of the leaves are reflected in the water.

far right Autumn fall at its best with dazzling red, orange and gold leaves of Japanese maples.

foliage colour

Autumn can be a spectacular time in the garden, with foliage in a range of colours, from purples and crimsons to gold and palest yellow. Some deciduous trees and shrubs merely turn a dull brown, however, so you need to choose the varieties carefully to get the best show. Even for a tiny garden, you are sure to find a shrub, climber or tree that will give a good display.

Why do leaves change colour?

below right This maple, with its bright yellow leaves, is a centrepiece of the autumn garden.

The prime cause is dying leaf tissue, but the precise factors at work are not fully understood. The chlorophyll levels, which give leaves the dominant green colour, fall, revealing previously obscured pigments, including red, orange, yellow and purple.

The red pigment is at its strongest now, in the autumn. All this is triggered by shorter days, reduced light levels, falling temperatures, and high winds. The degree of brilliance varies from plant to plant, and is influenced by autumn light levels, night temperatures, soil fertility, and the length of the preceding winter. So if the colours in your garden change from year to year, that is the reason why.

Even if the display varies annually, depending on the conditions, some trees and shrubs are a must for the autumn garden. One reliable performer is the katsura tree (*Cercidiphyllum japonicum* var. *magnificum*), whose leaves turn brilliant orange and then give off the scent of toffee as they fall to the ground.

The many forms of Japanese maple (*Acer palmatum*) are also perennially popular, and produce a variety of gorgeous rich colours. Some are small enough to grow in containers, and so are ideal for small gardens.

above Fiery shades of reds and yellows, set off by the low sun, lend autumn a vibrant glow.

left The woods are at their most beautiful in the mellow midday autumn sun – a good time to collect the fruits of the season.

autumn berries

A big display of autumn berries provides a striking seasonal note and also adds a range of colours, from bright red to yellow and white. In time most, except the toxic ones, will get eaten by birds. Meantime, as the autumn mists descend and then lift, they will reveal beautiful clumps of tiny coloured balls high up in the trees and down on the ground, attracting extra wildlife.

trees and shrubs

The best berrying trees include ash (*Sorbus*), which provide a range of coloured fruit and several specimens that will not grow too high. The slow-growing *Sorbus* x *kewensis* only grows 2.5m (8ft) high and 2m (6ft) wide, and its late spring flowers are replaced by bright red berries. *Sorbus cashmiriana* eventually grows much higher, reaching 8m (25ft), but it will take over 20 years to do so. It has white berries with a black dot or eye. If you have room for a slightly taller tree, try *S.* 'Joseph Rock', which has yellow berries that become rich in colour towards the end of autumn.

left Ensure that attractive rosehips are prominently displayed, so that they can be fully appreciated.

above *Sorbus cashmiriana* has a mass of tiny white berries, which hang down in thick clusters.

Among berrying shrubs, pyracantha is one of the most prolific, with berries in many bright colours. Barberries produce blue-black fruits, *Gaultheria* has strikingly coloured magenta fruits and popular cotoneasters bear berries in many different colours.

rosehips

Many roses have outstanding hips, these include *Rosa moyesii* and *R. rugosa*, which make excellent hedges and have large, rich red flowers. They are disease-free, tough and hardy, and grow extremely well in sandy soils by the sea. The purple-rose flowers of *R. moyesii* start opening in early summer. The light pink flowers of *R. macrophylla* are eventually replaced by incredibly striking, long hips. The climbing *R. helenae* grows 6m (20ft) high; train some stems to dangle out of a large tree so that they clearly display their orange-red fruit.

above Pyracanthas provide a mass of small flowers in the summer, and these are followed by richly coloured autumn berries.

left Roses are excellent all-round shrubs or climbers, adding colour, scent (with the right choice), and attractive autumn rosehips from varieties such as 'Hansa', which are full and red.

seedheads and bark

Many plants have wonderful seedheads, which can be just as attractive as flowers. *Clematis tangutica* and *C. 'Bill Mackenzie'* both produce large fluffy balls of silvery silk that look exquisite when lit by the sun, especially when growing up through a tree.

One of the few plants with brightly coloured seedheads is *Physalis alkekengi*, the Chinese lantern. This perennial has vivid red or orange "paper lanterns", which can be cut and used in dried arrangements. For a wildflower garden, teasel (*Dipsacus fullonum*) is a must: its shapely, architectural seedheads not only look imposing but provide valuable food for birds. Poppies and thistles also add interesting shapes to the garden.

above and below right Clematis provide some of the most exciting seedheads in the garden. Those of 'Bill Mackenzie' and *C. tangutica* are at their best when covered with dew or lit by the sun.

top right Grasses, such as *Stipa tenuissima* in a naturalistic planting, look good planted with late perennials and architectural seedheads.

end of summer and in autumn, exposing the most exquisite bark beneath which is patterned cream, russet and grey. In fact the eucalyptuses offer some of the fastest growing trees, many with excellent bark. Quite a few species of tree can be kept shorter than they would otherwise grow by coppicing or pollarding. Those with attractive bark include *E. coccifera* (grey with white), *E. deanei* (pale yellow, grey and hints of red), the crooked, multi-stemmed *E. pauciflora* subsp. *debeuzevillei* (mottled like *E. p.* subsp. *niphophila*, but peeling in patches, not strips), *E. fraxinoides* and *E. gresoniana* (both white), and *E. viminalis* (white and reddish-pink).

Stewartias are much slower growing, and the best include *S. pseudocamellia* and *S. sinensis*. Both have colourful bark which turns dark reddish-brown before it begins to flake, exposing the new bark beneath. The foliage on both also turns bright red before falling.

bark

If you visit any arboretum in winter you will quickly see how many trees have amazing bark. The range includes bark which keeps peeling back in papery scrolls, revealing fresh new bark beneath, such as *Acer griseum*, and trunks which have quite beautiful colours.

The most popular trunks are gleaming bright white, for example *Betula utilis* var. *jacquemontii*, and they are dramatic on sunny autumn and winter days. 'Grayswood Ghost' has glossy leaves, the fast-growing 'Jermyns' has rounded leaves and large catkins (pussy willows), and 'Silver Shadow' has large, drooping dark green leaves: all three have particularly brilliant bark. As the white bark gets dirty, which invariably happens, you can even clean it with buckets of hot water to bring out the striking colour.

Another tree that is well worth growing for its bark is *Prunus serrula* with its smooth, shiny, and dark brown mahogany trunk. It eventually grows to 10m (33ft) high. If you have room, grow *Eucalyptus pauciflora* subsp. *niphophila* which has shedding white bark at the

top left *Acer griseum* is a constant attraction with its peeling strips of bark.

above The wonderfully patterned bark of *Stewartia* is displayed as the surface peels away to reveal new colours underneath.

left As this cherry tree expands from the middle, the old bark starts to peel off in papery strips.

above A country garden with *Vitis coignetiae* over a pergola, *Parthenocissus* and chrysanthemums.

top right A gravel garden, with shapely grasses, looks good even at the end of the year.

above right Conifers come in a wide choice of colours and shapes.

opposite *Aster novae-angliae* 'Alma Potschke' and fennel glowing in the mellow autumn sun.

autumn ideas

It is a good idea to go round the garden in autumn and see which areas could be livened up with new plants. Start by simply ensuring that you have plenty of late-flowering plants, such as asters, chrysanthemums, dahlias and autumn-flowering clematis. Fuchsias also have a wonderfully long season.

Colourful foliage is another essential feature, especially on climbers, and a novel way of letting everyone see it is by training the likes of *Vitis* and *Parthenocissus* over a pergola. In fact the sensational colours are even more exciting when you are standing underneath, on a sunny day, looking up at the sky through a thick film of orange and red. However, gardens do not have to rely just on bright colours for interest. Areas covered in gravel with specimen evergreens and grasses chosen for their architectural interest add interest. They will be just as attractive in autumn as in spring and summer, perhaps more so if the grasses have beautiful beige flowerheads.

Conifers are also extremely useful, coming in all shapes and sizes from dwarf varieties to the pencil thin 'exclamation marks', which can be used to create formal Italian-style gardens. They can be used as dividers and focal points, and have a surprising range of different coloured foliage: all shades of deep or bright green, soft pale blue-grey, brilliant yellow and even coppery bronze.

Besides adding new plants, the autumn is a good time of year to see exactly where artificial constructs would add interest to the garden, including statues, pillars, pergolas and gazebos.

borders

All beds and borders need star performers for each season, providing a continuation of shape and colour. There are scores of first-rate autumn plants, including dahlias, cannas and Japanese anemones, while many grasses are now at their best. *Cortaderia* (pampas grass) has lavish plumes of spikelets in late summer and autumn, and is a magnificent eye-catching compensation for the absence of summer flowers.

Other grasses, such as *Molinia*, are not as immediately dramatic but their green strappy leaves will soon turn an astonishing orange-brown, and when they are placed to catch the setting sun look like they are about to ignite. Deftly placed contrasting yellow rudbeckias add an extra richness.

left Autumn-flowering heathers can be used to create a vibrant, many-coloured tapestry in the garden.

above When allowed to multiply naturally, cyclamen will in time produce a carpet of pink and white flowers.

left *Cortaderia selloana* 'Sunningdale Silver' looks stunning when planted against contrasting dark plants.

below *Molinia caerulea* ssp. *caerulea* 'Variegata' and *Rudbeckia* make an appealing duo in this perennial border.

bulbs

Autumn bulbs provide as much fun and colour as the spring ones, and can be spectacular when naturalized under trees or on a bank. One of the very best is the hardy *Cyclamen coum,* which flowers in shades of purple-magenta, pink and white. The most eye-catching forms include the red flowering 'Nymans' and the white 'Album'.

patchwork colours

Heathers provide a big boost to the autumn garden because they are still flowering when many border plants are dying down. Even better, they have different coloured foliage, and because most grow to a fairly uniform height up to 60cm (24in), they can be used to provide a flowing tapestry. Create a special bed with two or three focal points.

right Cloud pruning is a Japanese technique, stripping branches of foliage, leaving clumps at the end.

below Two strong, sturdy cones add immediate shape and style to this garden and will create extra interest during the autumn and winter months.

topiary

The moment the summer garden starts to fade, the key architectural ingredients start to grab the eye. And some of the best are topiarized shapes that range from traditional birds, urns and simple geometric shapes, to clouds, animals, chairs, and even cars.

do-it-yourself topiary

The best way to decide where to place your topiary is to walk round the garden on a late autumn afternoon when it is looking quite bare, and decide where it really needs livening up. Topiary invariably works best as surprise features. It is remarkably simple to grow your own. Start with a sturdy 30cm (12in) high *Buxus*

(box) cutting. You can prune it in the spring to the desired shape, or to make a spiral, wait until the plant reaches the height you want, then start making cuts. You can either cut it by eye, or use a piece of string and run it round the plant so that you have a line to follow. Thereafter trim once in the spring and autumn to keep it looking smart and stylish.

To make a more elaborate, intricate shape, grow the box cutting inside a strong 3-D frame. Get one made to your design by a blacksmith, or buy one ready made. Stand it over the plant, and clip the growth as it pokes through. Again, trim it twice a year.

You can also create a topiarized hedge, turning one into a battlemented wall with windows, doors and turrets. Some types of conifers, such as yew, respond well to being cut back and provide a dense,

even surface. If you want really quick results, however, you might consider using *Leylandii*, which grows at 1m (3½ft) per annum in its early years. It will make an effective topiarized shape, smooth and solid, but you will have to be prepared to clip it very frequently to keep it looking neat. *Cryptomeria japonica* is suitable for "cloud" pruning, a Japanese technique which can be applied to a range of shrubby plants. Prune the plant to leave a limited number of stems, strip off their lower leaves and create geometric shapes at the ends. You can even apply this to a *Leylandii*, reducing it to three or four vertical stems, each one having a ball of bright green at the top, swaying in the wind.

above Box can be clipped to create beautiful, stylish shapes.

left An inventive chair-shaped piece of topiary, with a flat base to sit on.

shapes, and classical Italian-style containers with decorative touches. One large container is important as a focal point, and elaborate ceramic or stone urns always have plenty of impact.

Modest terracotta pots can be given a new lease of life by painting them in different colours. Think carefully about which colours to use, since coloured paint can stand out quite differently from the colours of plants. Pots can be decorated to your own taste, perhaps with narrow or broad stripes, for example in blue and white, pale green and yellow, or with vivid speckling on a bright background. These colours will not be evident in the summer when the flowers and leaves bush out and hang down, but they will show from mid-autumn when they inject extra life to patios and terraces.

above Simple terracotta pots are the perfect foil for the bright pink cyclamen flowers.

right The muted blue-grey and purple of ornamental cabbage is given added interest by a shiny, galvanized steel container.

opposite A group of containers is used here to stunning effect with *Erica gracilis, Skimmia japonica* 'Rubella' and *Gaultheria procumbens*.

containers

The imaginative use of containers is an excellent way of prolonging the growing season. Many plants are suitable for an autumn display, including a wide range of evergreens, small deciduous shrubs (for foliage and berries), late-flowering perennials such as asters or sedum, bulbs and ornamental cabbages. Good choices of bulbs are cyclamen in small containers and cannas in large ones. Heathers and skimmia make good container shrubs and even certain maples can be planted in large pots.

Check that the pots are clean and attractive in their own right because now, in the autumn, as the plants start to die back and they are less lush and abundant, they can become a prominent feature. Stone troughs always look good even when the plants have died down. Galvanized steel containers and buckets add a bright, modern look, and look good with plants whose leaves turn reddish-purple, or evergreens with shapely, shiny leaves. If you can afford it, it is also worth investing in a few really attractive pots, such as Victorian-style pots, with their different

AUTUMN TASKS

This is an extremely busy time of year with plenty of important tasks. The garden needs to be tidied up before winter, with all the debris swept away. Beds and borders need a final weeding, tender plants need digging up to be put in pots over winter, perennials need cutting back from now to the end of the season, ponds need clearing out, and the vegetable garden can be dug over. It is also a time for planting trees, shrubs and bulbs. Note this year's successes and failures, and what you intend doing differently when next summer takes off again.

left Dead leaves, particularly large ones like *Gunnera*, which are less likely to blow away, can be used to cover any perennials that need protection from frost.

above Bubble insulation on the inside of the glass panes will save money if you heat your greenhouse during the colder months.

early autumn

The weather in early autumn is still warm enough to make outdoor gardening a comfortable experience. Although the vibrant flowers of summer may be gone, there are plenty of delights to be enjoyed in the form of late-flowering gems such as nerines and chrysanthemums, not to mention the bright berries.

Apart from planting bulbs, and protecting frost-tender plants, there are few really pressing jobs at this time of year. You should, however, move any evergreen shrubs that need repositioning. Also dig up and divide any overgrown and congested perennials. Make sure that you have enough clean pots when it comes to potting up the tender plants which cannot be left outside in the frost and the wet. Pay close attention to the lawn. Go over it with a fork, stabbing it with the prongs to aerate it.

Early autumn is also the ideal time to start planning next spring's display of bulbs in beds, borders and containers.

the flower garden

❖ Plant spring-flowering bulbs
❖ Take fuchsia and pelargonium cuttings
❖ Sow hardy annuals to overwinter (only in mild areas or if you can provide winter protection)
❖ Plant lilies
❖ Plant up a spring window box, container or pot with bulbs
❖ Clear summer bedding and prepare for spring bedding plants
❖ Continue to watch for pests and diseases on roses and other vulnerable plants
❖ Disbud dahlias and chrysanthemums as necessary
❖ Lift and store dahlias after the first frost
❖ Lift and store gladioli and other tender bulbs, corms and tubers
❖ Take in tender aquatic plants from the pond if frost is threatened

plants at their best

❖ *Anemone* x *hybrida*
❖ *Aster novae-angliae*
❖ *Aster novi-belgii*
❖ *Chrysanthemum*
❖ *Dahlia*
❖ *Hibiscus syriacus*
❖ *Nerine bowdenii*
❖ *Pyracantha*
❖ *Rudbeckia*
❖ *Salvia uliginara*
❖ *Sedum spectabile*
❖ *Sorbus*
❖ *Sternbergia lutea*

above You can pack more bulbs into a window box by planting in layers. Place large bulbs such as daffodils or tulips at the lower level and add potting soil.

above Position smaller bulbs such as scillas and crocuses on top of the larger bulbs. Try to position them so that they lie between the larger bulbs.

above Plant a container of evergreens for autumn and winter, and add some early-flowering bulbs to brighten up the display in late winter and early spring.

the greenhouse and conservatory

❖ Bring in house and greenhouse plants that have been standing outdoors for the summer
❖ Sow spring-flowering plants such as cyclamen, schizanthus and exacums
❖ Clean off summer shading washes
❖ Repot cacti if necessary
❖ Check that the greenhouse heaters are in good working order. Arrange to have them serviced, if necessary
❖ Pot up and pot on seedling pot-plants as it becomes necessary
❖ Plant hyacinths for early flowering under glass

above To plant lilies, dig an area of soil to a depth of 20cm (8in), large enough to hold four or five bulbs. Add coarse grit or sand.

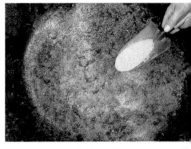

above Add a sprinkling of bonemeal or a controlled-release fertilizer.

above To preserve and store garden canes, knock off most of the soil, then scrub with a stiff brush and garden or household disinfectant.

above Collect old bedding plants to transfer to a compost heap. Being non-woody they rot down easily. Make sure that there are no seeding or perennial weeds.

above Space the bulbs about 15cm (6in) apart and make sure that they are deep enough to be covered with about twice their own depth of soil.

above Pot up a few mint roots to prolong the season and for early leaves next spring. Keep them in the greenhouse.

late autumn

A last-minute spurt of action is often needed at this time of year, to get the garden ready for winter and ensure protection for plants that need it. In many areas the cold will already have taken its grip, but in warmer climates there are still mild days to be enjoyed.

Besides tackling the many jobs described here, the autumn is also a good time of year to think of redesigning the garden. While most plants are dormant you can put up pergolas and arches, build walls, design new beds, lay paths (avoiding areas where they will get covered by leaves which become mushy and slippery in wet weather) and dig ponds. It is better that new ponds are left to be filled by rainwater over winter, thus avoiding the chemicals in tap water, which can lead to the growth of quick-spreading algae.

The autumn is also an excellent time to start ordering new seed catalogues. With everything still fresh in the mind, you'll know what needs to be grown where next year, what is not worth trying a second time, and which areas of the garden need to be spruced up.

the flower garden

- ❖ Cut down the dead tops of herbaceous perennials
- ❖ Clear garden refuse and leaves and put in the compost bin
- ❖ Remove pumps from the pond, clean and store in a dry place for the winter
- ❖ Plant bare-root and potted trees, hedges, shrubs and roses
- ❖ Clear summer bedding if not already done so
- ❖ Finish planting spring bulbs as soon as possible
- ❖ Plant tulip bulbs
- ❖ Protect vulnerable plants that remain in the garden
- ❖ Bring tender chrysanthemums indoors if not already done so
- ❖ Prune berry bushes
- ❖ Take hardwood and softwood shrub cuttings
- ❖ Prepare the pond for winter
- ❖ Remove leaves that have fallen on rock plants
- ❖ Cover alpines that need protection from winter wet with a pane of glass
- ❖ Protect the crowns of vulnerable herbaceous plants such as lupins from slugs

plants at their best

- ❖ Acer
- ❖ Berberis
- ❖ Cotoneaster
- ❖ Fothergilla
- ❖ Gaultheria
- ❖ Iris foetidissima
- ❖ Liriope muscari
- ❖ Nerine bowdenii
- ❖ Pyracantha
- ❖ Schizostylis coccinea

above After taking hardwood cuttings, dip the moistened base end of each cutting into a rooting powder.

above Plant hardwood cuttings over a layer of sharp sand, 8–10cm (3–4in) apart, leaving 3–5cm (1–2in) above ground.

above Lift clumps of chives and pot up for an extended season. Divide the clumps if necessary.

above Scrub old pots and containers inside and out with a disinfectant to ensure they are disease-free.

above Prune soft fruit bushes to about 23–30cm (9–12in) after planting. This stimulates new growth from the base.

the greenhouse and conservatory

❖ Clean and disinfect, ready for the winter

❖ Insulate

❖ Ventilate whenever the weather is mild enough. This is vital to keep air circulating and eliminate diseases such as botrytis, which flourishes in damp, still air

❖ Except with winter-flowering plants that are still in strong, active growth, gradually give plants less water. Most will then tolerate low temperatures better and disease should be less of a problem

❖ It is not too late to sow cyclamen seed for flowering the following Christmas

❖ Throw out empty seed packets, and give the greenhouse a final check, cleaning any equipment being stored away, especially spades and trowels

above After lifting chrysanthemums, trim the roots and then store in a tray with about 3cm (1in) of soil.

above Disinfect the frame and staging of a greenhouse, to prevent pests and diseases overwintering.

above *Cyclamen hederifolium.*

notes

Through trial and error, you can create the garden of your dreams, with the certain knowledge that you will have another chance to get it right the following year. Use these pages to record your planting successes and failures.

bulbs

Type ....   Planted ....

Variety ....   Flowered ....

....   Tip for next year ....

Type ....   Planted ....

Variety ....   Flowered ....

....   Tip for next year ....

perennials

Type ....   Planted ....

Variety ....   Flowered ....

....   Tip for next year ....

Type ....   Planted ....

Variety ....   Flowered ....

....   Tip for next year ....

below *Stipa splendens.*

grasses

Type ....   Planted ....

Variety ....   Flowered ....

....   Tip for next year ....

Type ....   Planted ....

Variety ....   Flowered ....

....   Tip for next year ....

shrubs

Type ....

Variety ....

....

Pruned ....

Flowered ....

Tip for next year ....

Type ....

Variety ....

....

Pruned ....

Flowered ....

Tip for next year ....

climbers

Type ....

Variety ....

....

Pruned ....

Flowered ....

Tip for next year ....

Type ....

Variety ....

....

Pruned ....

Flowered ....

Tip for next year ....

trees

Type ....

Variety ....

....

Pruned ....

Flowered ....

Tip for next year ....

conifers

Type ....

Variety ....

....

Planted ....

Pruned ....

Tip for next year ....

Type ....

Variety ....

....

Planted ....

Pruned ....

Tip for next year ....

above Dramatic autumn foliage is one of the highlights of the gardening calendar.

below Dwarf conifers planted close will gradually merge with one another to create a living sculpture. A spiky phormium provides strong contrast.

index

Page numbers in *italic* refer to the illustrations

above Scarlet red rosehips in early autumn.

Sira, 27br © Clive Nichols, 29bc, 32bl © Mark Bolton, 46tl © Steven Wooster, 47 © Meyer/Le Scanff, 53 © John Glover.
The publisher would like to thank the following people for their help in making this book: Beth Chatto; Bilboul Gardens, Earl's Terrace, London designed by Bowles and Wyer; Bosvigo House, Cornwall (p50b); Dartington Hall, Devon (Dartington Hall Trust); The Dillon Garden, Dublin (pp6–7); Fardel Manor, Devon; The High Beeches, West Sussex (High Beeches Gardens Conservation Trust); RHS Rosemoor, Devon (pp54–55), Sumil Wickes' Garden designed by Lara Copley-Smith (pp10–11, 50t); Liz Middlebrook, The Garden House, Buckland Monachorum (pp38–39); The Stonemarket Garden, RHS Tatton Park 2001 designed by Geoffrey Whiten (p51t); Westonbirt Arboretum, Gloucestershire (Forestry Commission), RHS Wisley.

The publisher would like to thank the following people for allowing their photographs to be reproduced in this book: Peter Anderson 1, 3, 4–5, 9, 13, 14bl, 15tl, 19bl, 21br, bl, 24tr, 26bl, 27tb, tc, tr, 28tl, 30 tl, 31, 32, 33, 34, 35, 36, 37, 38–39, 40, 41tr, 42r, 43t, 44tl, b, 45, 46tr, 48r, 54–55, 62tl, 63, 64. Jonathan Buckley 2, 20, 21tr, 28bc, 29bl, 44tr, 49, 62bl. Andrea Jones Jacket image, 23tr, 24tl, 25, 26tl, 30bl. Peter McHoy 56–61. Debbie Patterson 41b, 42l, 43b. Steven Wooster 6–7, 10–11, 19tr, 29tr, 50, 51r. Garden Picture Library 12bl, 17tr © Jerry Pavia, 14tl, 15r, 24tc © Howard Rice, 14tc © Neil Holmes, 14tr, 26br © JS

above Bright pyracantha berries in the autumn sun.